Sailors, Merchants, and Muleteers
of the California Mission Frontier

Jack S. Williams
Thomas L. Davis

The Rosen Publishing Group's
PowerKids Press™
New York

*To the people who transformed California through commerce and
who made it a little more comfortable for the settlers who lived there*

Published in 2004 by The Rosen Publishing Group, Inc.
29 East 21st Street, New York, NY 10010

First Edition

Editor: Joanne Randolph
Book Design: Corinne Jacob

Photo and Illustration Credits: Cover, p.18 drawings by Raymond Aker, courtesy of the San Diego Maritime Museum; back cover courtesy of Jack Williams; p. 4 courtesy of the Bancroft Library, University of California, Berkeley; p. 6 photo by Cindy Reiman; p. 7 drawing by Father Ignacio Tirsch, courtesy of the National Library of the Czech Republic; p. 10 courtesy The New York Public Library Department of Communications; p. 13 (1587 map) courtesy of the Bancroft Library, University of California, Berkeley, overlay drawing by Corrine Jacob and Thom Davis; pp. 16, 17 by Jack Williams; p. 20 Scala/Art Resource, New York; pp. 22, 26 Archivo Iconografico, S.A./CORBIS; p. 24 Hulton/Archive/Getty Images; pp. 29, 49 Photo Collection/Los Angeles Public Library; p. 30 © Fort Guijarros Museum Foundation, Watercolor by Jay Wegter. Fort Guijarros on Ballast Point, San Diego Bay, California, as it may have looked in 1800; pp. 34, 44 "Diccionario demostrativo . . . del Marqués de la Victoria", Museo Naval, Madrid; p. 37 The Mariners' Museum, Newport News, Virginia; p. © 40 Bettmann/CORBIS; p. 48 Culver Pictures; p. 52 illustrated by Jack Williams; p. 55 courtesy San Francisco Maritime NHP, A11 15,695.2N; p. 57 original art reference by Jack Williams, recreation by Corinne Jacob.

Manufactured in the United States of America

Contents

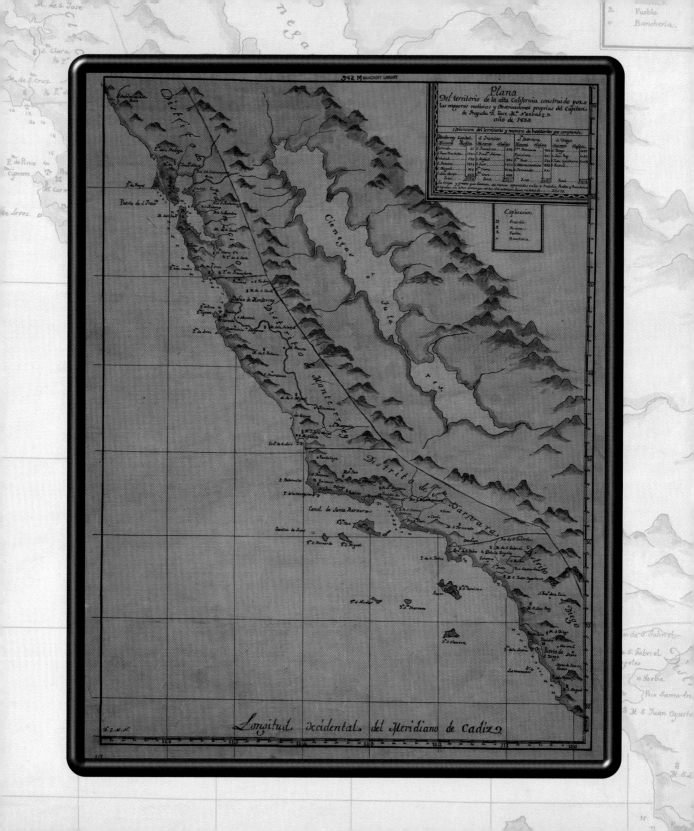

Plano
Del territorio de la alta California construido por las mejores noticias y Observaciones proprias del Capitan de Fragata D. José Mª Narvaez.
año de 1830.

Division del territorio y numero de habitantes que comprende.

Esplicacion.

Longitud Occidental del Meridiano de Cadiz

Supplying the California Frontier

In 1769, the Spanish Empire began the colonization of a long stretch of the western shore of North America. The section of the coastline that Spain controlled rarely extended more than 50 miles (80 km) into the interior of the continent. The remote province was called Alta California, or Upper California. By 1834, Franciscan priests, soldiers, and settlers had established a chain of 21 missions, four military outposts called presidios, and three small towns. The settlements that formed the links in the chain were surrounded by dozens of smaller ranches, Christian Indian villages, and farms. The distance from the northernmost settlement at Sonoma to the southernmost outpost at San Diego was a little more than 500 miles (805 km).

The most important Spanish settlements in California were probably the missions. At these frontier communities, a small number of Roman Catholic priests and a few soldiers attempted to transform the local Native Americans into Christian townspeople. Carlos III, king of Spain, hoped the neophytes, or Native Americans who were converted to Christianity, would support the newcomers living in the presidios and act as a military force that could help to protect California from the invasions of rival European powers.

In order to survive in California, the missionaries needed many things. Besides personal supplies, such as clothing, bibles, and writing tools, they

◄ *The territory of California was divided into four districts corresponding to its four presidios , as shown in this 1830 map of Alta California by José María Narváez.*

Trade goods, such as tobacco, tea, beads, and colored ribbon, were in constant demand in California. This is a block of tea that was imported from Asia. Pressing the tea into blocks made it easier to transport on trade ships or in packs on mule trains.

needed equipment to perform religious ceremonies. They also needed thousands of other things, such as tools, paper, seeds, blankets, soap, musical instruments, clocks, medicine, lighting equipment, pots, pans, and sacks. The Franciscans also wanted objects that they could give as gifts or as rewards for Native American cooperation, such as glass beads, tobacco and cigarettes, special foods, crosses, and ribbons.

Some things, such as basic food products, could be grown in California. Other items could be created using raw materials found near the missions. However, the only way to get many critical supplies was to bring them from the outside world. Most of the goods were transported to California by sea. Spanish sailors of the royal navy, and later foreign merchants, brought the items to California. Once the sailors arrived, specialists moved the supplies within the region using packs loaded onto the backs of mules. These men were called muleteers, or *arrieros*. The goods that came from

In this painting by Padre Ignacio Tirsch, a muleteer and his wife deliver cloth to a mission in Baja California. The woman is using a special saddle that allows her to sit sideways on the animal.

the outside world usually ended up in a store or a warehouse at the presidios or the missions.

This book presents a picture of some of the people who made it possible for the early Californians to get the supplies that they needed from the outside world. Without sailors, merchants, and muleteers, the missions and the other frontier settlements could not have existed.

Learning from Photo Studies and Maps

To understand the role of early sailors, merchants, and muleteers in California, we have to use a variety of information. No one can see into the past. To figure out what happened in history, we have to work as detectives. Many different kinds of researchers gather evidence. Cultural anthropologists study what living people do in order to figure out how earlier generations did things. Other researchers collect old stories and spoken descriptions of what happened. Archaeologists study the remains left behind by earlier people, including the ruins of buildings and broken pieces of pottery. Historians study the written records created by early settlers.

Some historians specialize in the study of photographs. These images often record changes that otherwise go unnoticed. By the time that most of the missions were abandoned, around 1840, the process of photography had not been invented. Nevertheless, pictures taken during the decades that followed can be very valuable for understanding the people who lived at the settlements during the mission era. For example, many old photographs show how frontier stores gradually declined. By using the photographs and other kinds of evidence, we can reconstruct how the stores looked when people lived in them.

Maps represent another important source of information. These documents are crucial to our understanding of how people came to and went from California. Old maps show us the routes used by early travelers. They also provide us with information about the colonists' understanding of geography. This field of knowledge involves the physical characteristics of the earth. For example, for many years Europeans did not know about the existence of the Hawaiian Islands in the Pacific Ocean. For more than 200 years, Spanish ships sailed far to the north and south of the islands without ever realizing that they were there.

The use of maps and photographs is especially important in our study of sailors, merchants, and muleteers. The evidence of these groups' activities in and around California consists of little more than written descriptions and crude diagrams. By carefully comparing these records to photographs and modern maps, we can sometimes reconstruct these pioneers' routes and even identify many of the special problems that they faced. In some cases, we can actually retrace their very footsteps.

Photographs and maps reveal important information
◄ *to researchers about trade routes that were traveled overland*
or by sea, as well as about a people's understanding of geography.

Why California?

Sailors, merchants, and muleteers came to California with different objectives. Some people came because they saw opportunities. Others arrived as part of their military assignments. All three of these groups shared one important trait. They all brought goods to California's settlers.

The most important goal of the Spanish navy and its sailors was to move supplies, information, and people to California. Military ships also helped to explore the region. They protected the coast from invasion and enforced laws that prevented foreigners from selling things to settlers. Sailors and naval officers helped to build many of California's settlements, including several missions. A few seamen served at the region's military bases, and a small number even became colonists.

Nearly all the merchants who came to California were foreigners. The main reason that these businessmen visited the region was to trade for animal skins that they could sell in other parts of the world for large profits. To do business with the settlers and the Indians, they brought goods from Europe and Asia using wooden ships similar to those used in the Spanish navy. After a while, some of the foreigners decided to move to California, where they set up *tiendas*, or stores, and other businesses. Before this, the

This modern map of California shows the trade routes used by Spanish settlers and those who traded with them. The dotted lines off the coast show the routes used by sailors. The dotted lines in the interior were traveled by muleteers and new settlers. The modern map is superimposed over a 1587 map from the atlas of Abraham Ortelius.

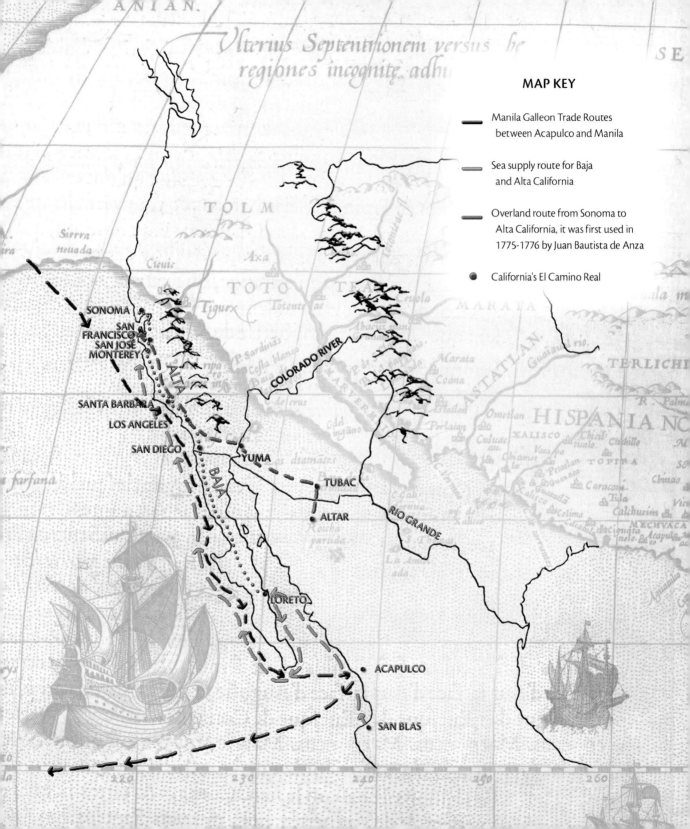

MAP KEY

Manila Galleon Trade Routes
between Acapulco and Manila

Sea supply route for Baja
and Alta California

Overland route from Sonoma to
Alta California, it was first used in
1775-1776 by Juan Bautista de Anza

California's El Camino Real

SONOMA
SAN FRANCISCO
SAN JOSÉ
MONTEREY

SANTA BARBARA
LOS ANGELES

SAN DIEGO

COLORADO RIVER

YUMA

TUBAC

ALTAR

RIO GRANDE

LORETO

ACAPULCO

SAN BLAS

only people who operated anything that might have been classified as a store were the Franciscans and the presidio commanders. No one else in the early mission frontier was allowed to sell goods.

The muleteers came to California to make a living delivering goods to the people who lived in the province's settlements. Officials at the missions or presidios usually paid them a small salary. Once they had moved to California, many of the muleteers raised families and took up other kinds of jobs.

The Spanish Navy

Spanish government officials relied on the royal navy to supply California's mission frontier. The Spanish fleet was made up of a combination of privately owned merchant ships and military vessels. However, nearly all the Spanish ships that came to California were under military command. It was the military ships, and not the private Spanish merchant vessels, that usually moved goods to California.

The Naval Department of San Blas

The Spanish navy had many bases all around the world. Some of the ships were assigned to ports in Europe. Other Spanish naval strongholds could be found in the Caribbean, in South America, and in the Far East. The ships that were assigned to California between 1769 and 1821 were almost all based in what was called the Naval Department of San Blas.

The headquarters for these vessels was the port of San Blas, in the modern state of Nayarit, Mexico. In 1768, King Carlos III created the outpost to serve Sonora, California, and the coast of North America as far north as Alaska. The heart of the base consisted of a shipyard where vessels were built, equipped, and repaired. The outpost had facilities that included offices, a church, warehouses, a hospital, and many workshops. The employees at the

The customshouse at San Blas, pictured above as it appeared in 1982, would have been a busy building in colonial times. Many of the shipments that were sent to California passed through this building.

facility also had homes and barracks in the town. A small fort protected the harbor. The base represented a small city with a population of more than one thousand workers. Unfortunately, jungles surrounded the port, and the people that lived there suffered from many tropical diseases. Of these, malaria was probably the most deadly.

The people who lived in San Blas included military sailors and civilians. The members of the royal navy were organized in a similar way to those in the army. There were high-ranking officers and regular seamen. Many of the

The customshouse at San Blas was used as a warehouse and an office for export. Here it is shown as it appears today.

This is an illustration of the Spanish ship San Carlos, *which was among the ships used to serve the missions and presidios of Alta California.*

people who worked in San Blas were civilians. These men were contracted to do a lot of the work onshore and even joined the regular sailors on their voyages in the Pacific Ocean.

Every man who served in the navy was a volunteer. The sailors of San Blas were recruited for service in Spain's other ports. In general, experienced seamen were chosen first. The sailors were short by modern standards. Because the decks of the ships were so close together, no one taller than 5 feet, 10 inches (1.8 m) was allowed to join the navy.

Few of the men who commanded the ships that sailed to California held the rank of captain in the Spanish navy. Most of the individuals were pilots. These seamen were not regular officers. They were civilians whose unusual skills earned them the responsibilities of running ships.

The people who served at San Blas represented many different races, nations, and cultures. The non-Europeans included Native Americans, blacks, and Asians. Some of the men came from Great Britain and the British colonies along the east coast of America. Perhaps the largest group of foreigners was the Irish. One of the three captains sent in 1769 to found San Diego was an Irishman named Callahan.

The people of African descent came to San Blas by many different routes. Nearly all the black people in the navy were born free. The first groups of Africans who moved to Spain had arrived between 700 and 1492. They came as part of the Muslim invasion of Europe. Many of these people eventually converted to Christianity. Their descendants formed an important part of the Spanish population. By 1750, there were many black seamen in the Spanish navy in the Americas.

Some of the royal navy's sailors were of Native American descent. These seamen came from families that had roots in many different regions of Spanish America, including Peru and Mexico. During the early colonial period, some of the Indians had joined Spanish crews to man the ships of exploration. Other Native Americans mastered the art of sailing during the centuries that followed. By 1750, many Native Americans worked on the ships of the royal navy.

King Carlos III, also called Charles, spent a great deal of his energy and wealth improving the Spanish navy and army. Francisco José de Goya y Lucientes (1746–1828) painted the king as he appeared when he went hunting, one of his favorite pastimes.

Some of the remaining people who worked in the Naval Department of San Blas came directly from Asia. Most of these men had ancestors who had lived in the Philippines. Spain conquered the Philippine Islands during the sixteenth century. By 1750, people of Asian descent routinely formed large portions of the crews of Spanish ships that sailed in the Pacific.

The multiethnic heritage of Spain's sailors gave the crews of the ships of the royal navy an unusual appearance. Foreigners were often amazed at the diversity that they saw on Spanish vessels. Although the sailors came from many different groups, they all spoke Spanish, had a similar set of beliefs, and worked for the Spanish Empire, whose king, Carlos III, ruled a vast portion of the known world.

Most of the people who served on the ships were men. The youngest members of the crews were cabin boys and gunners' helpers. The cabin boys were usually at least ten years old. They served as junior officers without pay. Warships usually had large numbers of gunners' helpers, who helped to man the cannons during battles. These children were called powder monkeys. During the fighting, they had to bring gunpowder from deep inside the ship's belly to the cannons on the upper decks. The powder monkeys were often killed during sea battles. If they survived long enough, they became sailors or gunners.

The most common kind of ship in the Naval Department of San Blas was a small supply vessel called a packetboat. Packetboats weighed less than 200 tons (181 t). They had two or three masts and crews that rarely numbered more than 50 men. From six to twelve cannons and swivel guns were usually used to protect each ship. The second class of weapons consisted of smaller artillery pieces that were used in hand-to-hand fighting. The crews of every ship were equipped not only with cannons but also with muskets, pistols, spears, hooks, and swords.

The largest ships in the San Blas squadron were described as *fragatas*, or frigates. These vessels were similar to the packetboats, except they were better suited for use as warships. Most of San Blas's frigates were equipped to act as transports and cargo ships. The smallest watercrafts that were sent north were

The 74-gun warship San Juan Nepomuceno
*was painted by Alejo de Baerlinguero. This vessel was built
in Guarnizo, Spain, and served in the fleet from 1766 to 1805.
Powerful warships such as this one occasionally visited California,
but were not assigned to the Naval Department of San Blas.*

goletas, or schooners. Some of these vessels were only a little larger than rowboats.

Nearly all the supplies and people that were headed for California passed through San Blas. During the Spanish era, every member of the community, including the soldiers and the civilians, was expected to help prepare lists of the items that they needed for the next year. These documents, which were known as *memorias*, were compiled by the presidio commanders and were sent to Mexico along with similar requests for goods that were prepared by the missionaries. Army officers and Franciscan officials in Mexico City purchased most of the goods based on these lists.

After they were purchased, the items bound for California were packaged in boxes, cloth sacks, barrels, and mats for their long journey. Every package was marked with a special symbol that indicated where it was going. Mules brought the supplies to the coast.

When the goods arrived at San Blas, they were inspected and then stored in separate government and Franciscan warehouses. They remained in San Blas until a ship was available to take them to California. Because it could take more than a year for the next vessel to become available, many of the items became spoiled or rotten. Most of the settlements received an annual shipment of goods. When the items arrived, the commanders had to create a detailed inventory, called a *factura*, describing all the things that were present.

Besides providing supplies to the California settlements, the Naval Department of San Blas was supposed to patrol the coastline and prevent enemy ships from attacking the province. During the mission period, which lasted from 1769 to 1835, Spain was at war at various times with Britain, France, and the United States. During these conflicts, the navy made special preparations for fighting and for protecting California if necessary. However, none of these enemies ever attacked Spanish California.

During the Mexican War of Independence, which lasted from 1810 to 1821, no ships were available to protect the region. The squadron of San Blas was needed to protect other parts of the Spanish Empire.

In 1818, a privateer sailing under the flag of the Argentine Republic attacked California. A privateer is a ship that is given a special license during wartime that allows it to attack enemy merchant ships. After a short battle, the privateer and its crew captured and burned Monterey before moving down the coastline toward San Diego. After raiding Mission San Juan Capistrano, the ship departed the province.

The Russians also moved into California during the Mexican War of Independence. They built a trading post north of San Francisco at Fort Ross

Fort Ross was an important trading post of the Russian-American Company between 1812 and 1842. This image was made in 1865, many years after the site had been sold to John Sutter.

in 1812. During the next two decades, teams of Russians and Aleuts from Alaska swooped down the coast, killing tens of thousands of sea otters. The sea otter pelts were sold in China and Europe for huge amounts of silver and valuable trade goods. Once the sea otters were killed off, the Russians turned to agriculture and raising livestock. Unfortunately, the Russian colony in California never met its agricultural goals, and the Russians sold the fort in 1841, several years after the mission era ended.

The Manila Galleons

The only Spanish ships that were not from the Naval Department of San Blas but that regularly visited California came from the Philippines. Since the sixteenth century, merchants in Mexico City had financed an annual voyage between Manila in the Philippines and Acapulco in Mexico. Chinese merchants secretly brought the Europeans many exotic products. The ships sailed each year carrying silk, spices, and porcelain in an amazingly long voyage that took them across the Pacific Ocean to Mexico and then back to Asia. The large cargo vessels were called the Manila Galleons, or *Naos de Manila*. California was an ideal stopping place along this trade route.

Although merchants financed the voyages, the king owned the ships. The government established strict rules about everything that happened on the voyages. Once the ships left Manila, the contents were sealed. The crews were not allowed to unload their cargo until they reached Acapulco. The sailors were not allowed to trade with anyone along the route. Although the

Theodor de Bry created this image of a Spanish galleon in the eighteenth century.
Between the sixteenth and nineteenth centuries, Spanish galleons sailed the Pacific Ocean
carrying exotic goods from the Philippines to Mexico and then back to Asia.
On the journey, the sailors sometimes stopped to visit the missions and presidios in California.

ships from the Philippines did not bring any supplies to the mission communities, the visits of the galleons caused a great deal of excitement among the people of California. They were more than twice the size of the largest vessel in the San Blas squadron, with crews of more than 300 men. The Philippine ships brought news from the other side of the world. However, for the most part, the visits of these vessels had limited effects on life in the colony.

Foreign Merchants

After 1790, a growing number of foreign merchant ships were seen on the coast of California. These seamen first visited the province during their voyages to the Pacific Northwest. On the coast of what is now Washington State and British Columbia, they sold their cargos of trade goods to Native Americans in exchange for sea otter skins.

Foreign merchants from the United States, Russia, and Britain soon discovered that the Californians, including the missionaries, were anxious to buy goods. At first, the inhabitants of the province offered the foreigners supplies of food and sea otter pelts. Later, they sold cattle hides to the merchants. Although this was technically smuggling and was illegal, the Californians gradually increased the numbers of exchanges that they had with these merchants.

Why did the inhabitants of California take up smuggling? Because the settlements of the region were growing rapidly, and the amount of space in the supply vessels was limited, there were always shortages of imported goods. At the same time, California's settlements, and especially the missions, had a large surplus of certain things. Cattle herds grew with amazing speed. After 1800, there was usually more meat and hides than anyone needed. By selling cowhides to merchants, the missions and settlers could get many things that

Hides from cattle that would be sold or used in trade were stored in buildings called hide houses. Foreign merchants built this hide house in 1823 to store hides for trade with the missions at San Fernando and San Gabriel. In 1829, the hide house was sold to Mission San Gabriel.

they wanted. The foreign merchants found so many people willing to trade them cowhides that they began to call the skins California dollars.

After 1790, Spanish government officials became concerned about the growing problem of illegal trade. Unfortunately, King Carlos III did not have enough men or ships to control the region's large coastline.

Despite their lack of resources, Spanish troops used ships to police the California coast actively. Between 1790 and 1810, they made it difficult for the smugglers to operate. In one confrontation, an American ship, the *Lelia Byrd*, fought a battle with the gun battery at San Diego. Many foreign merchants were arrested and jailed in San Blas.

In 1810, the Mexican War of Independence began in Mexico.

Spanish fort Guijarros, located on what would become San Diego's Ballast Point, was completed in 1797, after Spanish officials realized that they needed to be able to defend their ports. The only time that the guns of Fort Guijarros were fired was during the battle with the crew of the Lelia Byrd.

During the decade that followed, the government rarely sent any ships or supplies to California. As a result, the local officials tolerated, and later openly accepted, unlimited trade with foreign merchants. This period of free trade lasted from 1816 to 1821.

In 1821, Spain surrendered its control of California. The region was now a part of Mexico. The new government allowed the foreigners to trade in California. However, officials insisted that the merchants pay taxes on their purchases. By 1830, dozens of foreign ships could be found in California's waters. Some merchants even set up stores in the towns. Some paid taxes, but more often than not they found local officials who were willing to arrange illegal trade. The new republic tried to end the smuggling, but the nation lacked vessels or troops that could protect or patrol the coast of California.

Most of the merchants who piloted and financed the foreign vessels came from the emerging economic centers of Boston and London, though there was an amazing amount of ethnic diversity among the vessels' crews that came to California. Regardless of who worked on the ships, it was the merchants who stood to create or lose the huge profits that could be made from moving sea otter pelts and cowhides to the Far East and Europe.

The foreigners used many different techniques to trade illegally with the Californians. They sometimes visited presidio ports by claiming that they needed emergency supplies or repairs. While they were there, they tried to bribe local officials to allow them to trade. The smugglers also met townspeople, ranchers, and missionaries at prearranged, secret locations at the beach. Under moonlit skies the goods would change hands. After 1810, the Californians sometimes visited foreign ships to make their purchases. Some of the vessels were equipped like floating stores, with sales counters and display cases.

By 1834, the end of the mission era, California was becoming an important part of a new world of international commerce. Almost everyone in the region used goods that came to the territory through foreign merchants. The missions and many private ranchers, as well as foreign merchants, were able to grow rich from the largely illegal profits earned through smuggling. The missions would probably have continued to provide important markets for European goods had it not been for the government's orders that were issued between 1833 and 1835, which closed the settlements.

Life on a Ship

Life was difficult onboard the ships of the mission era. The sailors and officers had a hard life. They had to put up with many unpleasant sights and smells. Few modern Americans would be willing to live and work in such dangerous and cramped conditions.

The Parts of a Ship

The ships were the homes of their officers and sailors. The European vessels used during the mission period were complex machines with many different parts, rooms, and work areas. The upper part of a vessel included polelike masts, booms, sails, and horizontal beams called spars. The rigging included all the ropes and cables that were used to operate the sails, which actually propelled the ships.

The lower portion of the vessel consisted of the hull. Hulls were made up of planks, carved ribs, and various kinds of beams. The ribs were large, curved pieces of wood that helped to hold the ship together. Inside the hulls of larger ships were a series of decks made from beams and planks. Pegs held most of the pieces of wood together. The outsides of the hulls were usually painted to seal cracks and to protect the boards from rotting because of contact with the ocean water.

If someone went on a tour of the inside of a ship, he or she would find that the hull was divided into a number of sections. The rear, or stern, area of the ship housed the officers. Only the ship's captain had his own private quarters. The other officers were all crowded together into a room that was lined with narrow wooden bunk beds. When not on duty or sleeping, the men sat on benches at a large table in the middle of the room. This table was also used to serve food at mealtimes. Only officers were allowed in this section. Common sailors who came into this part of the ship without orders could be arrested.

The middle part of the ship consisted of a deep hole that cut through all the decks to the bottom of the ship. This hole was called the cargo hold. Here, freight and all the supplies required to operate the ship were stored. The bottom of the hold usually included a room with the ship's supply of cannonballs and gunpowder, and another tiny chamber that was used as a jail. Any sailor who broke the rules could expect to spend a few nights in this dark, smelly place. Near the hold, on the upper deck, was the kitchen area. It consisted of a large stove, usually made of bricks. The cook and his helpers worked in shifts in this hot space for 24 hours per day, maintaining their cooking fires. On longer voyages, animals such as pigs and chickens were usually kept in pens or crates near the kitchen. A massive wooden grate that prevented sailors and materials from falling in covered the upper surface of the hold.

The front, or bow, area of the ship was where the common sailors lived. These men usually slept in net beds, called hammocks, which were suspended

These drawings from a dictionary created by the Marquis of La Victoria show the hull of a Spanish ship. Notice the levels of the ship and the various rooms where men worked and slept or where cargo was stored.

from the upper decks. Sometimes wooden planks were also hung from the decks to serve as tables. The space set aside for sleeping was not divided into individual rooms. During the daylight hours, the men were expected to work there. Most of their time was spent making repairs to the ship, such as sewing sails and mending ropes. The sailors had no privacy whatsoever. No one made any attempt to bathe or wear any kind of cologne. There were no windows, and the air inside the hull barely moved. Because officers rarely visited this part of the ship, it was often littered with garbage. The bow areas that were the average sailors' homes were both unhealthy and uncomfortable.

The main deck of the ship was lined with cannons and equipment. The middle section of the deck, which covered the cargo hold, was left open. Short decks, known as the forecastle and the quarterdeck, usually covered the front and rear areas. A long rowboat was usually kept in the center of the main deck.

The darkest and most unpleasant parts of the ships were in the lowest levels of the hull. Here a person would find tons (t) of rocks surrounded by smelly seawater. The sails, masts, and rigging made the vessels top heavy. The weight of the stones helped the ship to stand upright. The rocks at the bottom of the ships were called *piedras de lastre*, or ballast.

Work Onboard the Ships

The operation of a sailing ship required a great deal of organized labor. The crews worked in teams called watches. The length of time that each group spent on duty varied. It was not unusual to have to work from 12- to 16-hour periods. During every hour of the day and night, part of the crew had to run the vessel. The ship's bell signaled the hours when one watch crew would replace another. A large hourglass filled with fine, white sand measured the time.

The sailors did many jobs. Some of the men were assigned to steer the ship and operate the sails. The sails had to be set and moved many times to get the vessel to go in the right direction. The ship was steered using a large wheel that was attached by ropes to a long board called the rudder at the stern of the ship. The voyage to California was especially hard because the winds that blew off the coast pushed sailing ships to the south. The only way that you could get to the north was to sail in a massive, zigzag pattern. It was very easy to get lost. The officers used a variety of charts and special scientific instruments, such as compasses and chronometers, to guide the ship.

Chronometers, such as this 1795 example made by Earnshaw, permitted correct measurements of longitude for the first time. Chronometers, compasses, and other instruments helped sailors to find their way to California.

 37

The wooden vessels built in mission times required constant repairs. Most of the men spent several hours per day scrubbing the decks with large pieces of sandstone. When any kind of a disease broke out, the officers had the men scrub the decks with soap, water, and vinegar. If a vessel developed a serious leak, or waves crashed over the sides, part of the crew would have to spend their time using a large pump that gathered water from the bottom of the hull and dumped it overboard. After a number of months at sea, the ships' crews were usually forced to beach their vessels and scrape off all the sea animals that had attached themselves to the hull. The most destructive of these creatures were sea worms. They ate the wood, creating leaks that could sink a ship. Every vessel had a special craftsman who used a combination of tar and hemp to fill in the gaps created by the worms.

Not all the work onboard the ships involved sailing or ship maintenance. Some men worked as cooks, carpenters, blacksmiths, and medical aids. A likely skill to be found on Spanish ships involved the use of cannons. Nearly half of every crew was made up of gunners. Some of the larger ships had individuals who were armed as regular soldiers. These fighting sailors were called marines.

The merchant ships that were owned by foreigners usually had smaller crews. As a result, they were somewhat roomier than most military vessels. Although they were owned and operated by merchants, their captains and other officers were given powers similar to those of military officials.

The men in charge of the ships had many jobs that did not involve sailing and navigation. They used cannons, flags, and pennants to signal other vessels and port officials. Every ship had a large, national banner. Smaller flags were used to signal the presence of disease, or even battle formations. Other duties included inspections of the men, the ships' supplies, and the freight.

The food and drinks that were provided to the regular sailors tasted awful. Sea biscuits, made from flour, water, and salt, were the mainstay of sailors' diets. After a few weeks, the biscuits were often filled with insects. After a few months of travel, the biscuits were transformed into piles of dust. According to their own accounts of life at sea, many sailors learned to like eating the worms, but discovered that the dust had almost no nutritional value. More than one crew turned to eating rats, ropes, or sawdust to fill their bellies. If they were lucky, the sailors might get a chance to eat a stew made from dried vegetables, such as corn, and dried beef. Occasionally, the men would catch some fish or a sea turtle and get a chance to enjoy a real feast. Before 1790, the sailors on Spanish ships often suffered from a terrible disease called scurvy, because they did not get enough vitamin C.

Bacteria quickly multiplied in the water that was loaded onboard the ships. It soon developed a disgusting flavor. Whenever it was practical, the sailors stopped at ports where they could refill their barrels with fresh water. On English and American ships, the men were usually supplied with large amounts of beer. On Spanish ships, some sailors occasionally drank red wine mixed with water. However, most of the time they had to make do with water.

In contrast with the sailors, the captain and the officers had their own special supplies of food and drinks. The captains often dined with some

 39

James Lind, a Scottish doctor shown in the above drawing, recommended that sailors at sea eat citrus fruits and drink lemon juice to prevent scurvy. This practice put an end to scurvy in the British navy. Citrus fruits contain much vitamin C, the lack of which can cause scurvy. Spanish ships also carried a supply of oranges, lemons, and limes.

level of elegance. The animals that were brought on longer voyages were kept for their tables alone. Typical meals included ham, cheese, and pastries. They also had private supplies of wine and other alcoholic drinks.

The exhausted men rarely had time for entertainment. When there was enough light to see, they sometimes carved wooden or bone objects. Some of the men used their spare time to shave their whiskers or to sew up the holes in their clothes. When they were allowed on the upper decks, the men fished, played music, and even danced.

Discipline and Punishment

The discipline that was imposed on the sailors was harsh. Men who violated the rules or slept too long could expect to be assigned many hours of extra duty. Minor violations were often punished with a stay in the ship's jail, deep inside the cargo hold. Serious violators were punished using a barbed whip. It was not unusual for men to die as a result of beatings by their officers.

Special Dangers

The sailors faced many dangers. The men who climbed the ships' rope ladders often fell to their deaths. Other seamen drowned while they were working on the ships' hulls. Sharks ate some sailors who were swimming, or who fell into the sea. There was also always the possibility of major storms, epidemics, or pirate attacks. Every sailor was particularly terrified at the idea of having to fight a serious accidental fire. Once it started, such a blaze was likely to end with the ship sinking. There were many special rules about crew members using lanterns or candles. None of the sailors or officers were allowed to smoke. No one was permitted to build a fire for warmth. Because of these orders, the men below decks were often cold, and they lived in semidarkness.

Medical Care

Every ship had a wooden chest filled with medicine. The officers used the cures of the period to treat the sailors who became sick. A few of the larger ships had surgeons. Most illnesses were treated using medicines and techniques that we now know did not help the patients. For example, cutting the wrist of a sailor to let the bad blood escape was thought to help almost any kind of illness. Many sailors died from the loss of blood. Broken arms and legs were often cut off. Because no one understood germs or the importance of cleaning wounds and staying clean in general, many people died from infections.

A Visit to a California Port

The sailors were always delighted when they finally reached a friendly port in California. The Spanish ships' crews nearly always stayed at the presidios. The officers allowed the men to go ashore, where they were finally given some measure of freedom. The settlers would have set aside an area inside the presidios for the sailors to enjoy themselves and sleep. The ships' officers usually stayed with army officials.

Most visits to California's ports were made to deliver supplies to the settlers. The boxes, bales, and bags of goods were lifted out of the cargo hold using ropes. Once onshore, the items were examined and then loaded onto mules for the trip to the warehouses. There the commander of the base made another set of inspections before filling out a report that listed everything that had arrived and its condition.

The foreign merchants who came to California were usually a great deal more rushed in their visits. They often used their long rowboats to bring goods to and from the shore. Most of the time, the exchanges took place at night, under a full moon. The missionaries and other settlers were usually just as interested as the foreigners in keeping their trading a secret.

Sailor Settlers

The Spanish king, Carlos III, decided not to build a major naval base in Alta California. However, many of the sailors who arrived in the province were given long assignments at the presidios and missions of the region. Most of the men worked as soldiers, although some were given special jobs in the building trades. Some of these seamen eventually decided to stay.

Throughout the mission period, a small number of sailors were commissioned to work at the presidios. Some of the men helped to repair the Spanish ships when they were in California. Others worked to build small boats for the use of the frontier army. Many of the sailors had training as blacksmiths or carpenters. They were often recruited to help build structures, such as churches and houses, at the missions and presidios. Sometimes several years would pass before they were transferred to another assignment.

Between 1769 and 1800, a sizable group of sailors was ordered to serve as part of the region's mission guards. These men worked shoulder to shoulder alongside the presidio soldiers who had the same assignment. A few of the seamen who lived at the missions chose to remain in California after their enlistment as sailors ended.

A large number of naval gunners helped to staff the coastal forts that protected the presidios after 1792. For a short period of time in 1793, some

Carpenters are building a ship in this drawing from the Marquis of La Victoria's dictionary. Sailors who settled in California often performed such skilled labor.

of these sailors were even placed in charge of their own small base at Bodega Bay, north of San Francisco. After they retired, many of the gunners found homes in California.

Other seamen were allowed to stay in California because they were seriously ill. The ships on which they arrived would have to continue their voyages. By the time the ships had returned, a year or two later, the sick sailors had often found places in the local community. The seamen were particularly expert in fishing and similar skills that were poorly known by most of the Californians. Governors and presidio commanders often argued successfully that these men should be allowed to retire from royal service and live as settlers in California.

When large groups of foreign merchants and sailors started visiting the region legally, many of them also decided to move to California. Between 1821 and 1834, a number of American and British merchants became Mexican citizens. Some of these men opened up stores and other businesses in the emerging towns. Other sailors became ranch owners or farmers.

The Muleteers

Muleteers were employed by the colony's military government and by the missionaries. They were responsible for transporting freight on the province's roads and trails. The early muleteers had the same kinds of ethnic backgrounds that were seen in the ranks of the Spanish navy. After 1800, many neophytes from the missions also took up this work. They had to train for several years to learn how to organize and move goods using mules.

Wagons, which were called *carros*, were rarely seen in California because the province had such primitive roads. Most of the settlements were given a few large carts with solid wooden wheels. These crude *carrettas* were used to haul cargo, including imported goods, for short distances.

The muleteers had to spend many hours making preparations for a trip. The mules were formed into long chains, called mule trains, which sometimes stretched for miles (km) across the California landscape. These trains could have from one dozen to several hundred animals. A great deal of time was spent putting the packs on the mules. If the animals' belts were too tight, the animals could be hurt and might not be able to continue the journey. If the packs were too loose, they could easily slip off, spilling their contents onto the ground or into streams or deep ravines. The lead mule in the train wore a bell. During various parts of the day, stops would be made to adjust the packs and

California settlers used crude carrettas, like this modern reconstruction, to move goods and supplies short distances. The carts were usually pulled by oxen.

to allow the animals to drink. During the late afternoon, the train would stop for the day. The heavy packs were removed from the animals' backs, and the mules were allowed to eat grass and to rest. At night, the muleteers slept either in the open or in improvised tents or huts.

California's roads were little more than pathways. There were no bridges. Every time the muleteers came to a deep stream or river, they had to unpack their loads and carry them across to the other side on their heads to prevent their freight from getting wet. When it rained, the trails quickly became so muddy that no one could move. Wild animals, such as wolves and grizzly

◄ *An arriero, or mule driver, keeps this mule train moving on its day's journey. Trains of mules were often more than a mile (1.6 km) long.*

 49

bears, often attacked the pack trains. Hostile Native Americans, storms, and stampedes were also problems.

The mules had a reputation for not cooperating with their masters. The muleteers were also known for their stubbornness and determination. Although these men often appeared to act cruelly toward their animals, the mules were almost always treated with care. Many muleteers spent a great deal of time treating sick animals. A good pack mule was worth more than twice as much as a trained horse.

The muleteers used the same kind of riding equipment as did the frontier cowboys. They usually rode tough horses furnished with sturdy saddles. Although they worked very hard, the muleteers were not paid as well as the soldiers or the sailors. Because the work was so difficult, many muleteers sought other careers when they had the chance.

While not working, muleteers' homes, families, food, and other customs were the same as those of the other settlers at the presidios and towns.

Warehouses and Stores

Most of the goods that were brought to early California ended up at stores and warehouses. The numbers and locations of these places changed over time.

During the Spanish period, between 1769 and 1821, the only places where settlers were officially allowed to purchase items were found at the four presidios. Each base included a general store, called a tienda. All the other imported goods were stored in nearby warehouses. Presidio officers operated the stores. They were paid a small percentage of the profit for their efforts.

Between 1769 and 1810, nearly all the missions' supplies also came into California through the presidios and were then sent directly to the Franciscan settlements. The majority of the goods were stored in warehouses until they were needed, or until the missionaries decided that they should be distributed to neophytes. Some of the larger missions built their own stores, where Native Americans and settlers could purchase supplies. The Franciscans operated the tiendas and kept the profits to purchase additional imports. After 1810, the missionaries bought most of their supplies directly from foreign merchants. They often sent goods to the presidios, whose stores and warehouses no longer received shipments from San Blas. Most of the time, the missions were the only place that the army could get supplies. The Franciscans supervised the operation of the stores in place of regular merchants or storeowners.

After Mexico took over California in 1821, some people living in the towns also built general stores. Many foreign merchants and wealthy landowners discovered that they could make a great deal of money selling goods to other settlers. Some companies that owned merchant ships also operated stores. Poor people who wanted to sell things brought their goods to marketplaces located in the open spaces in the middle of the settlements. Because these marketplaces had more goods, and there was competition between sellers, most settlers preferred to shop in the towns.

Wherever they were located, the general stores and warehouses had a similar appearance. The tiendas had large, wooden counters and shelves. The goods were stored in paper wrappers, mats, jars, wooden boxes, and barrels. The items that were popular included fancy cloth, chocolate, pottery, pots and pans, tobacco, playing cards, hats, needles, and scissors. The warehouses were long, barnlike structures. Because the food items were stored in the warehouses, rats and insects were a constant problem. Cats and dogs were enlisted in the fight against these hungry creatures. The doors of the warehouses and stores were often equipped with small, round holes that allowed the four-legged guards to pass freely in and out.

Because coins were scarce in the region, most of the exchanges took place in terms of credits and charges. Sometimes payment would be made in goods rather than in cash. The people placed in charge of the warehouses and stores spent much of their time keeping records of purchases and deposits. This job required mathematical skills that were rarely found among the frontier people.

◄ *This cutaway drawing is of a typical warehouse. It shows the kinds of items that were stored to be sold in the tiendas, such as grains, pottery, various foods, and tobacco.*  53

The Heritage of Early California Commerce

The Spanish sailors, muleteers, and foreign merchants who came to California between 1769 and 1834 changed the region forever. The Spanish navy was the first organization to bring in goods from around the world. The foreign merchants were the first group to export California's products to markets in Europe and Asia. Both the sailors and merchants depended on the region's muleteers to move the goods within California. Without these three groups, it is hard to imagine how the colony of California, and its Franciscan missions, could have survived.

A careful examination of the routes that brought goods to and from California indicates the extreme importance of the sea in the development of the region. Ships brought in almost everything that arrived in California from the outside world. They took away every product that left the region. The patterns of maritime trade and commerce that were established in the mission period, between 1769 and 1834, have persisted to the present day. The region is still tied by the ocean to the larger community of Pacific Rim nations, including China and the Philippines.

The lack of a reliable land route to California had important effects on the history of the region. Whoever ruled California needed a navy and supply ships. When Mexico took over the area in 1821, the new nation's lack of

This drawing of San Francisco in 1846–1847 shows that after the mission period ended, California continued to rely on the ocean for trade. Ships continued, and still continue, to follow trade routes along California's coast and to make stops to buy and sell goods in California's harbors.

these resources made it possible for foreigners to move there. Once citizens from the United States, Britain, and other European nations made their homes in Mexican California, foreign governments became seriously interested in conquering the region. In 1846, only eleven years after the last mission was closed, the United States completed this objective.

All the men who built the commercial links to, and within, early California deserve to be remembered. They set in motion the first steps of the economic development that has made California one of the most important commercial areas of the modern world.

San Francisco Solano

San Rafael Arcángel

Presidio
de San
Francisco

San José

Santa Clara de Asís

Pueblo de San José

Santa Cruz

Pueblo de Branciforte

San Juan Bautista

Presidio de
San Carlos
de Monterey

San Carlos Borromeo
de Carmelo

Nuestra Señora de la Soledad

San Antonio de Padua

San Miguel Arcángel

San Luis Obispo de Tolosa

La Purísima Concepción

Santa Inés

Santa Bárbara

Presidio de Santa Bárbara

San Buenaventura

San Fernando
Rey de España

Pueblo de
Los Angeles

San Gabriel
Arcángel

San Juan
Capistrano

San Luis Rey
de Francia

Presidio de San Diego

San Diego
de Alcalá

Glossary

anthropology (an-thruh-PAH-luh-jee) The study of human behavior, beliefs, and culture.

archaeologists (ar-kee-AH-luh-jists) Scholars who study the remains of peoples to understand their behavior.

cargo hold (KAR-goh HOHLD) A term used for the large hole, found in the middle of most ships, that was used for transporting freight and other supplies.

carrettas (kar-ET-ahz) Crude wooden carts that were used to haul cargo short distances in and around the Spanish settlements of early California.

carros (KAR-ohs) Wagons that resembled those used by American pioneers during their movement west. Because of the lack of roads, carros were rarely used in early California.

cultural anthropologists (KUL-chuh-rul an-thruh-PAH-luh-jists) Scholars of anthropology who focus on the study of living peoples.

factura (fak-TUR-uh) A list of received goods.

fragatas (fra-GOT-uhz) Frigates; small, swift vessels that could be equipped as warships or transports.

frontier (frun-TEER) The edge of a settled country, where the wilderness begins.

galleons (GA-lee-unz) Ocean-going ships equipped with sails.

goletas (goh-LEH-tahs) Small sailing ships that could be used to scout enemy positions or to move small amounts of cargo or crew.

gunners (GUH-nurz) Men who specialized in the use of cannons.

hammocks (HA-muks) Net beds that are suspended from a beam.

hull (HUL) The lower portion of a ship, including its outer wooden shell.

imported (im-PORT-ed) Brought from another country for sale or use.

marines (muh-REENZ) Special forces of fighting men who were armed and equipped to fight on land or sea, and who were normally assigned to ships or the navy.

markets (MAR-kits) Places where people exchange goods or services.

memorias (meh-MOR-ee-ahz) Memoirs; in California, this term was used for supply documents that indicated a settlement's requests for the annual shipment from San Blas.

multiethnic (mul-tee-ETH-nik) Of, relating to, or reflecting diverse racial, national, or religious backgrounds.

Naos de Manila (NOWS DAY muh-NIH-luh) Special Spanish cargo ships that carried Chinese goods from Manila in the Philippines to the port of Acapulco in Mexico.

outposts (OWT-pohsts) Settlements, small forts, or places that are far away from other places.

packetboat (PA-kit-boht) A kind of sailing ship designed to carry small amounts of cargo.

piedras de lastre (pee-AY-drahs DAY lahs-TRAY) Ballast; stones found at the bottom of a ship's hull that were put in place to prevent the ship from falling over.

privateer (pry-vuh-TEER) An armed ship licensed by a government to attack enemy ships.

province (PRAH-vens) One of the main divisions of a country.

remote (rih-MOHT) Far away.

rigging (RIG-ing) Ropes, chains, and cables that were used to control a ship's sails and masts.

rudder (RUH-dur) A long board, located at the rear end of a ship by which is steered.

smuggling (SMUH-gling) Sneaking something into or out of a country to avoid taxes.

stern (STERN) The rear end of a ship.

swivel guns (SWIH-vuhl GUNZ) Small cannons that were used to protect a ship or fort from attacks at close distances.

watch (WOCH) A team of men assigned to a specific period of duty aboard a ship.

Resources

There are many places where you can learn more about early California and the daily life of sailors, muleteers, and merchants. The following lists provide information about some of the more important resources.

Books:

Mora, Joseph Jacinto. *Californios: The Saga of the Hard-Riding Vequeros, America's First Cowboys.* Doubleday and Company: Garden City, New Jersey, 1949.

Wilbur, C. Keith. *Picture Book of the Revolution's Privateers.* Stackpole Books: Harrisburg, Pennsylvania, 1973.

Museums:

No single museum in California or the western United States focuses on trade or seafaring in early California. However, a number of institutions have exhibits that offer some information about these topics.

La Purísima Mission State Historic Park. *This museum has an amazing living history program that includes presentations related to commerce within the mission system and trade with the outside world. More information about scheduled living history events can be gained by calling (805) 733-3713 (www.lapurisimamission.org).*

Many other mission museums display items that were imported to California and provide some information about early trade.

Web Sites:

Due to the changing nature of Internet links, PowerKids Press has developed an online list of Web sites related to the subject of this book. This site is updated regularly. Please use this link to access the list:

www.powerkidslinks.com/pcm/sailmerc/

Index

About the Authors

Dr. Jack Stephen Williams has worked as an archaeologist and historian on various research projects in the United States, Mexico, South America, and Europe. Williams has a particular interest in the Native Americans and early colonization of the Southwest and California. He holds a doctoral degree in anthropology from the University of Arizona and has written numerous books and articles. Williams lives in San Diego, California, with his wife, Anita G. Cohen-Williams, and his daughter, Louise.

Thomas L. Davis, M.Div, M.A., was first introduced to the California Missions in 1957 by his grandmother. He began to collect books, photos, and other materials about the missions. He has, over the years, assembled a first-class research library about the missions and Spanish North America and is a respected authority in his field. After ten years of working in the music business, Davis studied for the Catholic priesthood and was ordained for service in Los Angeles, California. Ten years as a Roman Catholic priest saw Father Thom make another life change. He studied at UCLA and California State University, Northridge, where he received his M.A. in history. He is a founding member of the California Mission Studies Association and teaches California and Latin American History at College of the Canyons, Santa Clarita, California. Davis lives in Palmdale, California, with his wife, Rebecca, and his son, Graham.